Steeped in imagery and memory, Renée Nicholson's moving third collection *Feverdream* conjures a West Virginia simultaneously past, present, and perpetual. This is the land that holds not just Nicholson's dearest memories of her late brother, Nate, but also his very way of seeing and being in the world. Home, Nicholson reminds us, is more than a place or even its people—it is a quality of attention, an exchange of care, a mutual beholding. *Feverdream* feels like a gift, an invitation.
— Jonathan C. Chou, MD, author of *Resemblance/與*
(2024, Saturnalia Books)

"Can you taste a place / in its harvest?" the speaker of "Shenandoah Valley Gold" asks. And yes—yes you can in Nicholson's poems, which harvest treasures such as home in West Virginia, the body, loss and grief, classic films, aging, worry, and wonder. These poems stretch elegantly between Nicholson's characteristic golden serenity, but also her crisp, silver clarity. This is a poet who reaches fingers toward the sun while also keeping toes touching the humble Appalachian earth.
— Natalie Homer, author of *Under the Broom Tree* (2021, Autumn House Press)

Feverdream

Poems

Renée K. Nicholson

FEVERDREAM

ISBN: 979-8-89933-012-4 (Paperback)
Library of Congress Control Number: 2025924192

Cover Design: Erin Mann
Artwork: Sally Jane Brown
Book Design: Erin Mann

Printed in the United States of America.
First printing 2026.

Redhawk Publications
The Catawba Valley Community College Press
2550 Hwy 70 SE
Hickory, NC 28602
https://redhawkpublications.com

This book is dedicated to those called to the work of poetry, especially in the face of illness and in medicine, and for those called to the work of narrative medicine.

Table of Contents

Foreword

Arriving at "Karted" (nine poems deep into reading *Feverdream),* I found myself facing a delicious readerly dilemma: torn between wanting to speed up to consume the next sensorial poem and yet, simultaneously, wanting to slow down to let the current poem digest. In narrative medicine parlance, *the text was working on me.*

In this, her third collection, poet Renée Nicholson transports us to core spaces (*Home, Body, Loss, Seasons, Glow*) while mapping new routes between observation and experience, practice and progress, interrogation and reconciliation. Some poems relish local flavor; others ascend toward what's celestial or reverential. Some are as grand and stately as peacocks; others are swervy-swift as go-karts. Ultimately, Renée's poems serve:

> "There are places
> you don't refuse biscuits" and
>
> "Shame
> on those who curse the cold,
> the sweet sign we're still alive.
> Feel it under your ribs, pulled
> into the sacs of your lungs.
> That moon, diminished,
> yet the wind remembers,
> howling as if to say we are not lost.
> I pull words from the traveling
> clouds before they move on,
> or freeze in the mud."

Last year, while wading through a loss/grief situation that seemed too big to comprehend let alone traverse, I confided my overwhelm to Renée. She listened without interrupting and offered space for me to be heard. A few weeks later, I received a poem she had written, a dose of narrative medicine in the form of cinematic escapism (see "Upon Watching North by Northwest I Am No Longer Young"). It was then that I knew that Renée's poems belong to part of a broader emerging narrative medicine oeuvre. From an artistic perspective, they move in a way that parallels a dancer's improvisation. Thematically, they humanize much of what would otherwise baffle us or elude us altogether. In *Feverdream*, every disease is a rare disease -- that is, as rare as the person who carries the weight of the diagnosis.

This toggling between the particular and the universal balances narrative pride…

Diagnosis Color-By-Number
I bare my wolf teeth, curly lipped
smile. It has been said that the ill
are wounded in body and voice.
This is true, and not. I run
the doctor and nurse into my
wilderness. That's not quite it
either, but I'm shapeshifted,
wolf-girl, rejecting the hero journey
punted out of my teeth-bared story.

…and narrative humility:

Last Communion
Then, the bottom fell out—
nothing literal—and we stood
around a metal, outdoor table:
cookies, biscuits, homemade
dips with scoop chips, knowing
this would be the last…
We cleared the plates, went separate ways,
and I wondered, where would so many
young souls scatter? The bread, the body.

As the formal field of narrative medicine nears its third decade of pedagogy and practice, I invite us to both respect its roots and make way for new branches. This is not a matter of pure sustenance or aspirational dominance, but one of sustainability. The rigor and relevance of the narrative medicine movement will depend on how its core principles (attention, representation, affiliation) manifest themselves in its multivalent practice by its growing community of practitioners.

So…who *are* the people in these narrative neighborhoods? Many narrative medicine practitioners are certified clinicians; however, just as many are not. Thus, this: welcome to the poets, artists, musicians, chefs, photographers, architects, historians, sculptors and educators; welcome to the radical listeners and close readers, those who dare to join in the co-creation of this narrative community of knowing, of being, of creativity and catharsis that is both malleable and magnificent.

As you make your way through *Feverdream*, know that you are not alone.

In narrative solidarity,

Derek McCracken
International Narrative Practices Association
Lecturer, Columbia Narrative Medicine

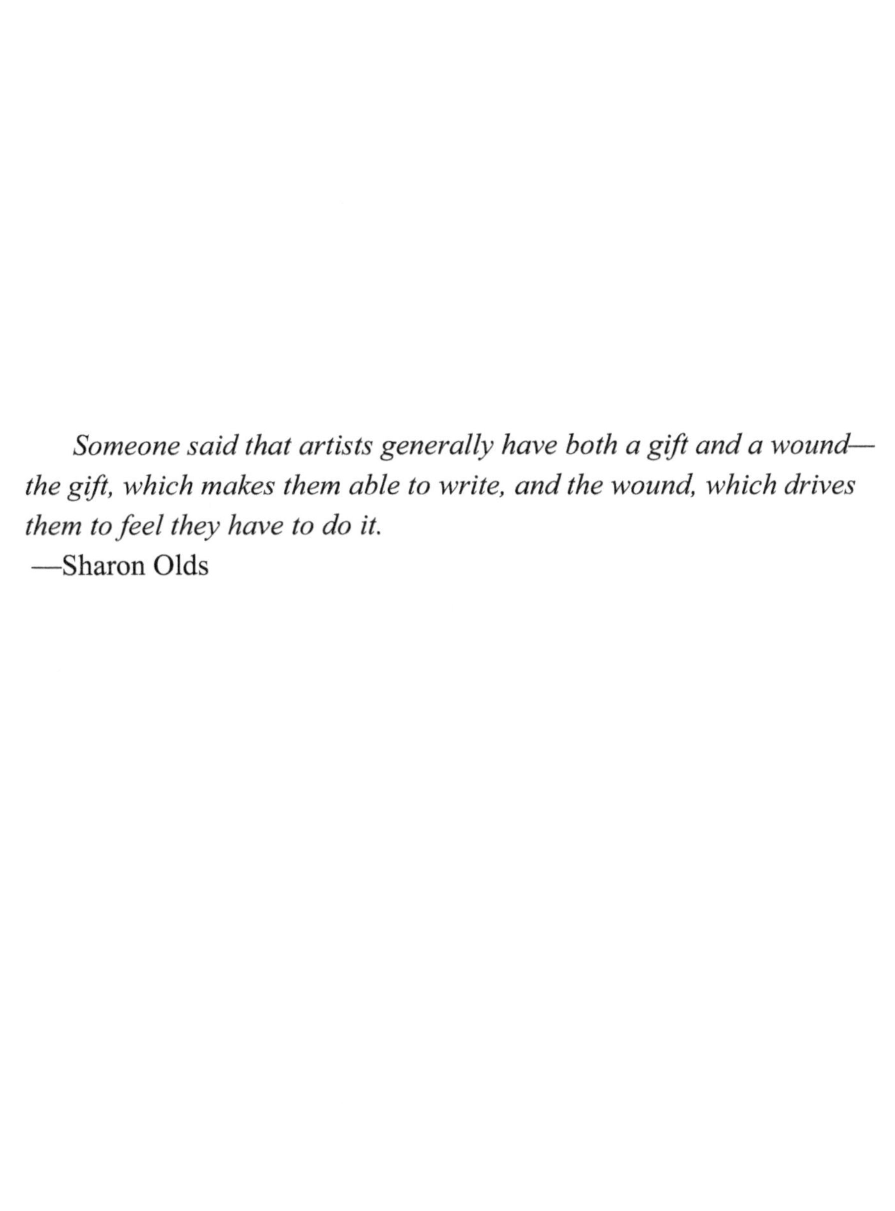

Someone said that artists generally have both a gift and a wound—the gift, which makes them able to write, and the wound, which drives them to feel they have to do it.

—Sharon Olds

HOME

Home

Another Poem About West Virginia

Cascading sky tears, the ones
I did not shed, the ones I wish
to cup in my dirt hands and make
a milky mud. In streaks, the sun
through the gap, ridge drenched,
saplings bowed in deep prayer,
supplicant of a fearsome god
I do not know. A distant
rumble suggests another downpour.
This place I refuse to leave,
my valley. Flood. Flood.

Regional Dialect

My neighbor
rides his mower downhill, once told me
that's how he knows. Still calls me
the Parkersburg girl
after twenty-odd years. We porch sit
and swap lies. Other neighbors throw
treats to my dog. We grow maples
and oaks, the chestnuts long gone. Can tomatoes,
make chow chow, pickle eggs. When the wind
rattles through, the haints might come. I tell them
come back when they can't stay so long.
I'll see them again one of these first days.
Ghosts always return, wisp-selves
floating into the dark sky
until they, too, become stars.

Lost River Heart

The beige and brown
of it, like late autumn,
sand and rock. We climbed
to Cranny Crow, surveyed
an undulating land wishing
to go fallow. I wore
my Lost River heart
like a locket or a talisman,
cool stone at my collarbone.
The sun high, hot,
while a single fuchsia
thistle stood at attention.
If you could wish on blue
sky, the day was yours.
The day was mine, wishing,
wishing, the wind shaking
the green and gold leaves
as if to say fall,
as if to say fly.

Shenandoah Valley Gold

–for Ryan McCarthy

Because the skin of the apples
bright, as if gilded, beckoned
my teeth tear
that bright skin, the crunch
its innards juicy, sweet—
you can taste the earth
lime in the dirt
coaxing the trees to bear fruit.
Can you taste a place
in its harvest? Orchards grow
in valleys surrounded
by a sentry, mountains
that feel like they've been stationed
here since the beginning of time. In
town, the giant, red apple statue
serves as a capsule, to tell
future generations
I don't know what.
But maybe

if we are lucky, if
we keep our bounty
there will be apple growers, pickers
in that future, that harvest, another
golden delicious time we can imagine.

The Humility of Ramps

The most pungent
among the onions,
My cousin Bill
pulled these wild
ones from a patch
beyond the yard.
He'll dry and chop,
mix in a bit of sea salt,
make a seasoning. Dominique
will pack up her girls,
drive an hour south
to the yearly dinner.
Three hours east, a gourmet
flatbread place serves them up
with asparagus. Not bad
for a wild thing, once
mistaken for a weed.

Under And Again

–for The Simulationists

A seam in the bituminous coal like a vein in the body and I'm told
this land is old and that we are an old people with old ways but

I am not yet old and when the spring redbuds start to explode the
hills bright fuchsia there is nothing so old about it

and if you stare at a place long enough you might find surface clues
to what's underneath. Once I dug a brick up in the yard

from a road that no longer runs through this patch of earth gone
like the chestnuts and the seam of black gold, the ceaseless

churn we call progress and then I saw the bluebird in flight and it
was marvelous.

Riverfront Timepieces

Luck ran like a slow
flowing river, despite the rain.
I threw myself into it, but
of course, I didn't. A thin
sun trickled beams
rips in the seams. Aren't we
such broken-down folk? The smell
of rain, or bread in the oven, sizzle
of sautéed onion. I sliced
the radish. Things of earth
can cure you if you let them. Drips
from the tin roof, like in a novel,
the dime-store variety.
There aren't any of those left. Think
of me in those peacock blues, setting
sun sinking into the uneven ridge, where
the night critters begin to stir. Trees twist
in the purple dusk, that muddy river pushing
nothing but tarnished pennies.

Some Road or Another

Sun high as I rolled
past, dreaming of what
might happen on the other
side, somewhere in America,
or what used to be.
And I looked at the houses, out buildings,
barns, the little farms, wondering
about the lives there: triumphs, heart
aches, bacon and eggs, crisp fall
apples, holiday feasts, humble dinners.
Clouds rolled past too, the sun
cresting, falling, fading. Asphalt
black and blank unfurling.
It stretched forever—
but it didn't. The rolling green hill
the trampled grass, a blur in the window.

Karted

There was always that dirt track, round
and round, the carts made of this
and that, whatever we could find,
duct tape for everything else.
Where did we think we could go?

Those shrieking peacocks
on the failed farm down the lane.
Who has a farm on a mountainside,
anyway? We drove like mad,
possessed, and the moon itself
egged us on, a checkered flag,

LIGHTS OUT. And every pore
of my being sucked in the night air,
I might have even taken flight—
the night sky open,
open.
Open.

Easy, Against Easy

There are places
you don't refuse biscuits.
Lean into the gravy,
consequences be damned
because you can be healthy
come Monday. If the sun
is high but starting to weaken,
order the extra coffee. It will warm
at midday. The mountains in fall
burst into color patches
mending clothes
with whatever they got.
Find your particular
spot, russet or persimmon, or
move on after the snap
of your camera. Buy a bag
of local apples, the ones
crossed with galas, learn
about the mother apple sharing
her sweet with her offspring. Or so says
the pine-knot man who sells them, who

heaves a half-bushel with little effort
or sweat. The paper bag crinkles
in your hands, as the sinking sun lights fire
to the pine needles, as if threaded with candles
soon snuffed out. Why can’t life
always be this easy? Once
I might have moved away, but the pull
invisible, like dark magic, reels me back.
Home. Such comfort, such burden. We don’t
talk about it, not talk-talk. Just like
the Virginia creeper, bluebirds and crows, goldfinch
and hawks. The volunteer squash makes
great soup. Sit—
stay a spell. Warm away your cares.
Morning biscuits
straight from the oven.

Gameday at the Taproom, Or How I Learned About the Football Voodoo Doll

–for Dave Housley

She waves a ragdoll in the air
blue, gold, gold-n-blue—
hat and shirt and big-bead necklace
matching, sure in her conviction
it brings luck. "Flag. Oh shit."
Maybe the next set of downs.
Room full-up with fans, not
even 100 bodies for
football or beer, ball-n-beer
take your pick. On top
of the big mountain, the town
focuses on tourists, summer
people and leaf peepers,
later, skiers. However you make
your dime. Early fall's russet
patches freckle the ridge,
night's crisp and clear like Kolsch
served up, begging firelight.

Easy sippin', but four
and out—
she won't close her tab, not yet,
libations for her and offerings
for the doll, afternoon
shadows tinged gold, all things
gilded, even superstition.

Make, Glow

West Virigina moon, shining platter
like the kind Gran served
biscuits on, made glow
the dark street and reminded me
of shadow corridors in Edinburgh,
where the alleyways seemed the only
way. And I wasn't afraid, even
as the wind kicked
because it wasn't any different
from Dutch Run or Wind Gap
in November or March when
the wind and rain-snow parted
and the calm settled in,
stars peeking through
misty clouds and your voice puffed
in wonder
Would ya look at that?
The train whistle and
the light in the window
tell me I'm home.

Home
Home

BODY

Body

Against Sarcopenia

It is a wish, wistful
full of fancy, to be swathed
in the full blues & turquoises
of many peacocks. Such is my lust
that no other greens
but emerald will do. Fine
colors feverdreamed, decadent,
one might even say royal,
flanked by filigree, glittering
gold. Not a dream of youth
but full-on middle life
where wisdom is folly
and folly is rich.

Clinical

All the furniture pushed
to the walls, a bare expanse
of industrial-grade blue. Wounded,
a voice crackles. Warbles.
No posters of organs or reproduced art.
An exam table the sandy-
beige of deserted beach, paper
covering the plastic cushion,
as though it matters.
Nothing approximates comfort. Wounded,
a voice cannot convey a story, but outside
the ridge disappears behind a wet curtain,
slick droplets on the windows. A wound
not a voice but a hushed-up, water-streaked view.

Diagnosis Color-By-Number

I bare my wolf teeth, curly lipped
smile. It has been said that the ill
are wounded in body and voice.
This is true, and not. I run
the doctor and nurse into my
wilderness. That's not quite it
either, but I'm shapeshifted,
wolf-girl, rejecting the hero journey
punted out of my teeth-bared story. Turn
it inside-out. Colors pour out of me, thick
lines of blue, yellow, red, muddied
together, thick and brushy and mad.
Not rainbow and yet not despair. Wild
beauty is still beauty—
wind blowing off a summer storm,
lightning clearing the ashen sky in bold streaks:
bright, mighty, and without remorse.

Ekphrasis/Menopause

I never saw Vermeer's women until
I became bloodless. Paused, gone from red
always hot and cold, pulled through a fog
that settled in the night, vision
changed. The woman in blue cast next to a map,
her blurred face less distinguishable from those young
women staving off suitors and unwanted advances.
Wine goblets to crimson mouths. Blue
murmurs, reading aloud, unaware.
She's the only one who sees
me because I am now her.

I Was Quite Outside My Body

Not floating, exactly, something akin
to watching a movie of myself. My
skin like taffy, pliant in a way I never
knew before. My shoes scraped cement
sidewalks leading nowhere. No breeze
shook the trees, and I walked this nowhere
for what seemed hours. Maybe time ceased.
I heard but could not see the running
water, its soft gurgle as it sliced and skipped
over unknown stones smooth from the incessant
lapping. Omens or prayers,
it was the immense knowing
of pure blue sky.

The Problem of Translation

The Germans have a word
for everything. *Libensmüde*
offhandedly translates to suicide
but that's not quite right.
"Life weary" is closer, like gloomy
winter days in succession.

But I like the days of winter,
find each one contemplative, in
its own gloomy way, which is not
gloomy at all. It can also mean

"careless," which seems not quite
weary of life. *Freitod*, on the other
hand, also translates to suicide,
supposedly,
but can apparently also mean
"free choice,"

not reckless like *Libensmüde,* which
in German, can also be used to say, “Are you
crazy? Do you want to get yourself
killed?” Carelessness, of course
is quite a different state.

Grilled

> **“Now is the time, my friends, to test our souls.”**
> **—Rober Hedin, “Transcanadian”**

Seduced by the sizzle
of meat, juices pooling
on the plate, the sun hiding
behind errant clouds, or
so we find them—
our great wish for brightness.
I am unable to swallow, not
quite a choke, the lump lodged.
Are we still talking
about the meat?
Abundance, or its lack,
how it is the third day
of rain, storms from nowhere,
bulwark of steely clouds forged beyond
our maps. Maybe love shriveled,
shook us loose, or once too many
times, left us drunk-like, and punchy,
and drained. Water doesn’t quench

what parches us, dust in our musty
souls. Instead, we make muddy
puddles, nothing delicious to spare.
Take the meat
before it spoils. I lack
appetite.

PicturePoemRx

–for Molly Humphreys

She wields a long prism,
part healing crystal, part
magic wand, and in the blink
of her shutter, captures
a trace essence, a hidden
whisp of spirit you never knew
you had. Images reflected,
refracted, light through the wand,
the makings of visual song. I search
for words to describe them
picture poems—
they resist. Like the doctor,
whose black leather gladstone
leans against the mossy
tombstone, now scribbling prescriptions:
levothyroxine, metformin, losartan.
The cryptic language of healing,
Latin mass, not unlike a poem.
I scribble to save a scrap

of something essential, but it slips
beyond us. Perhaps the attempt
is really the cure, our bit of sorcery,
a communion that binds us
where we don’t seek treatments, but pursue
the small flash of what it means to be whole.

Midlife Run On

When the needle skipped
right at the part of the song
where Prince does that screech-wail
only Prince can do, I tried
to jump like I did thirty years ago
in my old dancer's body and I didn't
so much rise into the air as groan
into a half leap that slumped earthward
and landed with a thwack-thud that was nothing
like a funky bass line or a sick guitar lick,
like the one in "Kiss," and—oh my—
right then I knew this new
threshold meant I fell
squarely into late middle-age,
listening to Prince as though
still young, partying like it's 1999.

I Try Not To Think What I Might Say

These nights, word-locked, key
to my memories lost, a closed-in
dust motes kind of darkness settles.
One baleful note, a train's whistle,
or the boiling kettle—not eerie
silence but a mundane lull
of treacherous, ordinary sounds
as day slips seamlessly to dreamless sleep. No
clouds but no stars, just dark, pillowed-
in blackness, deep, unwavering,
as if a hole swallowed us up
and we failed to notice.

Body

LOSS

Loss

All This That Came Before Now

I forgot to tell you
how burdened we were
with hope. Even
as he administered Nate's drugs, cleaned
the bathroom, and the body of his son,
Dad wished hard for a miracle, prayed.
A reprieve would have to suffice.
Tumors scattered, a scan overlapping, waiting
in the small hard box, my phone.
Yet, we found ourselves
in those hallucinatory days
of hospice, not the end,
but close, when Nate believed
he might still get better because he didn't
feel crummy. Sometimes I wondered
how many weeks
or months of travel
I might make—
I tell you, it was like this:
I watched him fade
as the hot Atlanta sun
drained out all color.

Floats

3 A.M. and Nate
wants a root beer float.
I make it, scooping,
plopping creamy balls
in pint glasses from which
we once sipped brown ale.
When we were kids
we begged for A&W,
made frothy floats,
drank them like they
were spun air, nothing at all.
Nate is seven inches taller
but the same weight as me.
He can't tell day from night,
but I'm his big sis, supposed
to look out for him, and all
I can do is pour IBC over
vanilla, find the long spoons.
After he's gone, I'll turn 50,
with my melted vanilla
and a totally useless scoop.

At 3 A.M. the rest of the world
is still, star-blanketed and dreaming.
Awake, I see all the world,
and nothing at all.

Kairos

If I see Nate in the squash, why
do I take a knife to it? Because,
it's what he'd do, season it
with garlic—how he loved
its bite and tang, the blend
of fleshy veg—sauté it in butter
before it goes to soup. I talk
to Nate in the kitchen,
it's all slice and sizzle, singing
along to Retro Cocktail Hour
feel it in my muscle,
my bones, and the tingly
nerves. My body prefers
facing the old
cutting board—scarred and nicked
from a thousand chops and slices,
heating my cherished Le Creuset,
though any pan might do—
to anything else. The knife,
a direct line to my brother's voice:
Remember thyme,

rosemary. Garlic.

Always garlic.

School Shooting at My Brother's Alma Mater

I almost said, "He'd die if he knew."
The hard crack of the piston,
the soft swish of palm fronds
in the breeze. Hunkered students,
waiting, their electronic messages
the tether to what is, what isn't,
what will be. Wescott Fountain,
center of the old campus, bubbles
in perpetuity, a brick placed for someone
already dead, because this was supposed
to be his happy place. Somewhere
even good memories turn cruel.
A law student previously survived
a South Florida shooting, now asks
how many more? There's quiet after
death, a quiet the surviving know.
It carries a tragedy that lies in wait:
the photo that pops up on your phone,
uninvited, or the card tucked in a drawer
that surfaces for reasons you can't
explain. I cried at the headlines,

was glad he never lived to know the ringing
after a bullet is fired and the silence broken.

Last Communion

Then, the bottom fell out—
nothing literal—and we stood
around a metal, outdoor table:
cookies, biscuits, homemade
dips with scoop chips, knowing
this would be the last. The horizon
slipped into nothing, evening
slant light, the kind to walk home in, before
the amber glow of near-night approached.
We cleared the plates, went separate ways,
and I wondered, where would so many
young souls scatter? The bread, the body.

Atmospheric River

I wandered a path through
the manmade woods today.
Baseball and softball diamonds
abandoned for the season. A soft
wind rustled a few brown leaves
and the reservoir, skirting
the far side, water-level low
despite the rain and snow,
blown through on another fast-
moving system. Now they call
them atmospheric rivers. The sky confuses
me, the gray comforts, sunshine
reminds me of that day
on the deck, my brother's first
week in hospice—I almost write
"care" but it's the wrong word.
I ugly cried, my skin
burnt beyond-pink
in the unrelenting Georgia sun.
Today is nothing like that. Two geese
cleave a path through the sky,

silent, even as earlier I endured their racket,
honking from above as I sipped tea.
Tonight, the moon will rise over bare
limbs, the trees not quite illuminated
as if dancing in a shadowbox. I contemplate
joining them, my arms waving
in odd angles and primitive forms
as though I'd never learned the discipline
of ballet. But I did. We shed our past lives
to live again. I wandered a path
through the woods of my own making,
my skin still pink, not red from a sun
I don't particularly want to see.

Can't Find You For The Stars

I thought showing up
might be enough—

a lousy word
for I wish or I thought or—

Maybe it was the afghan Mom
crocheted in garnet-n-gold, mottled
by the dogs, by you.

Grief is the sum total of my mistakes
minus that cloudless night we searched
the sky. You pointed a bony finger:

"There. Right there's where you look
for me." But,

nights cloud over
and my eyes are aging, and I—

lack a map and a compass,
can’t find you for the stars.

Still, I fold into your blanket,
my protective crust.

Upon Watching North By Northwest I Am No Longer Young

–for Derek McCracken

Cary Grant just dove
into a stand of corn stalks,
dust clinging to his sharp
gray suit, when I get a message
from a friend who lost
two siblings last year. One expected,
one not. This summer, my only brother
will be dead five years.
So much and so little
time. The Hitchcock Blonde
is never who she seems, perfect
cat-eye lid and pale lips. We move
between two worlds, celluloid flicker,
and the atmosphere here below, where
the cereal-and-steak lives march on.
I don't know what to tell my friend.
Growing old feels thin. My brother and I
told jokes about becoming shuffleboard champs
at the old age community. Instead, I watch

Tippi Hedren run with Cary Grant across
Washington's nose, or is it Eva Marie Saint
across Lincoln's? All dead, along with my friend's
siblings and my only brother, and yet some hope
glows brighter than my big screen TV, like an ember
lost from the underworld, or overworld, whatever
world exists beyond. I compose my response, vowels
all wrong, *I'm sorry* long and bland. Instead, I wish
to extend my hand to his, clutching our feeble dreams.
On screen, Cary Grant's gestures say
what words never could.

My Father's Pens

On the day the clutter
became too much, I
went at it, trash bag in hand.
Rows of them, sentries,
each smooth polished shaft
his favorite. An array of maroon
and emerald, midnight and graphite.
My father's perfect cursive
lines and loops. Lefty,
yet he never smudged
the flowing ink.
His pleasure in writing
the word, if not the word itself.
The heft in his hand, and
I am left to wonder
with what pen
he wished to say.

I might have casually swept these treasures
off to the dump: the Montblancs
& Pelikans, the trusty Cross & Watermans,

the ornate Omas & sleek Pilots. What shame—
carried by this writer-daughter
of such a collector (might
we even say connoisseur?)
Would I swallow it whole for losing
such an intimate and artful set
of writing implements?

My wordlove continues.

Perhaps, in some yet unknown feverdream,
a shadowy night filled with snow,
my own scribbles, written bit
by bit with my father's pens—I stop,
clean each apparatus
with a soft cloth and something
like prayer,
more thoughtful words
to scratch forth.

B&W Photo, 1955

My father's Uncle Darrell,
lanky, lean, as though he might twitch
into being again. I don't know
much about him. Granddad
lent him a Studebaker
so he could get a job. The dead
hold secrets but also tell stories—
his unbuttoned shirt reveals
a white undershirt. Cuffed pants.
In the '50's, he was neither a young
nor an old man. In 2025, I'm
not young either, caught in digital
photos in a bright pink sweater.
I keep Uncle Darrell's picture
on a bookshelf in a wooden frame,
where he beckons: remember
if not me, the idea
of who I once was.

Lost Fruit

–for Bill Parsons

Paw paws rotting
on the ground.
Wasted, the worst
of sins, so says
my Granddad, my Great
Great Uncle Otho,
my Great Aunt
Eloise, my Great Grandma
Lily. You can't grow
them, but if you
get them ripe, it's
banana meets mango
meets deciduous
forest. So many
rotting, as if
we missed our
chance to gather
in such sweetness.
Can you remember

the flesh? Which
relative gone
was known three
counties wide for
her paw paw ice cream?
Cold and sweet and
pure. All memory is now.
I didn't have the patience
to learn, to turn
the crank, to make
from our land,
to conserve,
by which I mean
to love.

Balance Sheet

Running a deficit
where I take more
than I give, or give
more than I take.
This is not economics,
you cannot graph
the heart. Except EKGs.
But it's that's not what
I mean. A robin keeps
attempting a nest
in the eaves
of my front porch.
I clear it. Yet day
after day that bird returns
building anew, undeterred,
despite running a deficit.
Our instincts don't
always run rational,
and I am more like the stubborn
robin, building nest after nest,

with blind hope
one might stay.

Supernova

The large cardboard box—
the kind used for moving wardrobes—
stuffed full of my old pointe shoes. Dirty,

spent, beautiful. Toe box softened, there was a time
I learned to hop delicately atop those tips,
to lift, and while aloft,

touch the clouds. When I opened my eyes
I wasn't so earthbound. My eyelids
didn't try to shut out that light. Sparks,

bursts, all I never did, or
tiny explosions, pressure, faraway stars.
The box, the dirty shoes, all still there.
Still,
here.

Once

The sky turned cotton-candy
blue-hued and pink-sweet
spun by a sun not yet set. A curve
in the highway revealed an abandoned
farmhouse tucked in a valley's crook
of interstate. When built, of course, no such
road existed. Sun-washed, two stories,
weathered brick, vines up and down
its battered bones. Windows missing,
one shattered like cracked teeth. Once
it must have been grand—two wings,
white columns to welcome
visitors and inhabitants alike.
A fresh, red-bricked haven
in a fortuitous dip of land. So many cars
and trucks speed by without a glance. Soon
the sky will purple into the night, and maybe
the ghosts will inhabit this once-grand country
house, its days of glory past. Light leaking through
the vacant window, where a candle
once glowed, welcoming someone home.

Loss

SEASONS

Seasons

A Scorched Feeling

This heat's all wrong:
creek too low—
should be filled
with rainwater. A scorched
feeling, yet it's not midsummer.
Late spring nights
should cool, but don't,
and a hazy sun that's not due
until July blazes in April.
Fatigue bones, a lazy
hazy way of being, or
an omen that must be bad.
An oil can cast by the roadside, dark
smoke billows up a stack. Soon
all there will be is cracked
earth and dried stones
where water once flowed.

Saturation Point

Decker's Creek flooded
its banks, water rushing
towards the lazy Mon meandering
up to Pittsburgh. Naked
tree limbs reached over
the brown water, casting spells,
while the rain continued
a relentless fall. After
the dry summer, the dry
autumn, the creek bed, dry,
cracked mud like earthen veins
devoid of blood, and everyone lamented.
"So dry I don't even mow the lawn." Maybe
all this wet was all we needed.
I felt the cold drops in succession
leaving their damp trace
on my cheek,
soaking into my coat.
They traveled the leafless branches,
rolled to the rocks,
sloshed the road, into the rushing

creek. I’ve been told the winter

is hard, but I saw it rush with life,

with water overcome,

washing away more than we wished to lose.

Approaching Autumn

Like a raised flag
the scarlet tree among
those still summergreen
signals some warning
about what is approaching
or receding. It's windmill-tilted
light falls autumnward, as do I. The heat
refuses to leave, lasts longer
than it should. This tree proclaims
the new season in hues impossible
like a runway model crossing
a busy gray street. Maybe I am
blazing bright toward the new
season before we've left the old. Harbinger
of cooler days and crisp nights, of first
frosts and hearty vegetables, of early
nightfall and cold rain,
trees resplendent before going
bare. Night of fire, mornings
of fog, the big face of a harvest
moon's glow.

Wintering

If the nightsounds
can't rouse in me
the words to write,
I ask you, what will?
The last full moon
of the year has come
and now receding, darkness
has the last say.
Earth muddy, soggy promise
in the time of sleet. Shame
on those who curse the cold,
the sweet sign we're still alive.
Feel it under your ribs, pulled
into the sacs of your lungs.
That moon, diminished,
yet the wind remembers,
howling as if to say we are not lost.
I pull words from the traveling
clouds before they move on,
or freeze in the mud.

Catch and Release: Stillness

Lake water ripples below iterations of
fluffy white and steely clouds
fighting for position, shading
the still-green leaves of hillsides
flanking the banks. A short row
of boats, tethered, tied, waiting,
but not exactly still. No one goes
anywhere but a lone pontoon,
with its low engine rumble
in a no-wake zone. Light breezes
incite tiny waves. Light shifts
as dark clouds blot the high
afternoon sun. The quiet of smoothed stones
lining the shallows, covered
by silt. A feeling of rain
without drops, nothing disturbs
the stillness, as if time
stopped, suspended.
No rain. Rain.

Spring Bouquet

The daffodils bow shriveled yellow heads
toward the muddied ground. I had been thoughtless
with someone's feelings,
a guilty endless drizzle of cold rain
after days of unseasonable warmth, unclothed
shame, like the wrinkled, contracted flowers,
once powerful for their pop of color.
I don't always know how to say I'm sorry,
slogging this way and that, soaking.
Other flowers will bloom, the white dogwoods
and the flamboyant peonies. I pull up
desiccated daffodils, tie them into a bouquet,
the only kind fit for saying forgive me.

May Day

Some ancient celebration, when spring
begins its tilt into summer, but today's breeze
and sun harken back. Still, I didn't gather
flowers, didn't dance
around a pole festooned with ribbon,
didn't weave garlands, didn't ignite
a bonfire. No May Queen, no Dionysus,
no Aphrodite. Just sun warming my skin
and maybe a lightness in my step.

1972

Watergate, the Munich Olympics, the first
scientific calculator, Bloody Sunday in Derry.
The year I was born, there were more VW Bugs
sold than Model T's ever manufactured. The Equal
Rights Amendment failed again, an avalanche
on Mount Fuji killed nineteen people.
But also: Apollo 16 achieved record speed
with the lunar rover, and don't you wish
you knew that wheel-crunch
over the moon's pocked surface?
Hurricane Agnes blew through, Curtis Mayfield
released *Superfly*, the Troubles in Ireland
pressed on. Bobby Fisher: Chess Champion,
Oakland A's take the Series. Before I am
born, lunar missions cease, yet I keep staring
up at moons and moons.
On Earth, we light candles on cakes, make
wishes only to blow them to smithereens, catalog
who was born and who died, who got sick
and when and with what. Where
did wonder go? I cannot tell you why

my birth year matters, except
it’s how I keep count,
all those many moons between,
how the same awful and wonder
somehow, hand in hand, march on.

What We Do in the Golden Hour

–for Chris Plein

The sun stays late
as we tilt southward
and raise golden
pilsner in thick glass
mugs. Cold beer, good
conversation—

a way to be in communion

which, if you think about it,
is kind of the point. That sun
wouldn't set for a good while.
I spied a white rabbit
hanging out in the yard
waiting for the bright moon, whiter

glowing, reminding me
all is not over when the day flips,
and night is never as dark as we
imagine it to be. Just remember—

Feverdream

Sometimes I wake deep in the night wondering
why I saw a red-tailed hawk, or why people are cruel,
sometimes about words I almost know. I fall back
asleep but keep that feeling of nearly
understanding some secret:
why a dog sniffs a circle before hunkering,
what the noisy geese say as they fly
towards the reservoir, or the crows that hang
like a gang from the electrical wires, or
that one shoe that had been buried in the yard.
There are bits we aren't supposed
to know, all those little unknowns flung up
in the middle of the night.

Seasons

GLOW

Glow

Simple Gifts

Fabric cool to the touch,
vinegar-tinged
pickled eggs, drinks naturally
sparkling, the last purple
of sunsets. The soft fur,
my dog freshly washed,
and the big moon nights.
A good hat on a sunny day.
The feel of coolness by
a mountain stream, raspberries
on the tongue. A perfect-ironed
pleat, linen and cotton and wool,
the first touch of skin to skin, dancing
cheek to cheek, the sound
of your voice when I'm far
away, but the sound of your voice
always pulls you near.

Gratitude, After Ross Gay

Start
with sorrow or loss, the equal
and opposite
of gratitude and delight,
or joy,

Of which he is particularly fond.

A pair of my grandma's earrings,
paste—but nice—converted
to post for my pierced ears. Smell

of soup simmering on the range,
the clear rounded sound of Miles,
Kind of Blue, vinyl,
of course. Just music and our
scratches.

The soft feel of my dog’s ears
after a good shampoo, my gratitude,
the soft sound of rain
on the roof like a lover’s

whisper: I’m here, right here.

The Art of a Child

–for Amelia Mick

A sun can be weary, it's whiskers
fanning ennui, needing clipped. A purple horse
stands in profile, and Mona Lisa smiles at you.
Such a tableau forms a cohesion—
a world where order isn't the same as sense,
which is more a sensibility, and why
wouldn't it be? In the art
of a child we are bestowed with what we once
were, face those dreams we didn't chase, a crackled
world where the odd takes up the mantle of normal
and the normal slips from view. In this art,
we're always with whom we might have been.

Making a Famous Picture

They'd wanted Steve McQueen.
(Who wouldn't?) He wasn't available.
Chose Peppard, who strutted
around the set like he was the star.
Cat was six different felines:
walking cat, sitting cat, kitty
drenched in the rain. That party?
Improvisation by card-carrying
actors, not extras, the last take
with real champagne.
The nonnegotiable clause was Hubert
and his exquisite black dress—standing
dress and walking dress—and "Moon River"
an octave plus one, her range.
Overbearing husband banished
from the set, and no more notes
on her performance. She didn't need
them. She was already luminous.

Lobby Bar

The old place opened
again. Chandelier lit
as if out of a classic movie.
Or what I imagine them to be,
all those celluloid dreams.
Reclined in your tulip seat,
darkened, quiet, a place
to talk of nothing in particular,
watching a cascade of bubbles
dancing up the flute. You smiled
like old times, like Robert Redford,
light glinting off cut class. Outside,
rain threatened—
the weak sunlight not yet dusky. Inside,
shadows, a scrim hugging a half-lit
rosé evening. We took
our time, barkeep poured another.

Viewfinder

Have you ever seen yourself
in some old picture, surprised
how time and space allow
for a cool remove? Perhaps
you gained weight, or lost it,
spot gray in your hair and how
you got older but somehow looked
young? A shade of lipstick or
an article of clothing brings out
an aspect you all but overlooked,
and now can't stop yourself.
Is it vanity that draws you in, or
for the first time does your gaze
mimic how past loves once
saw you, their filter like a magic
scrim? We never touch the world
through the pads of our fingers,
sense cool rain on our skin. We
see the world through mimeographs,
a split second caught in our hearts,
myriad lifetimes—maybe we could

know no other way—and smooth
our battered experiences
in a single click.

Song for the Curious

From my chair
in the dimmed
front room I see
the back window
of my neighbor's
house glow with soft
yellow light. Shade
drawn, I have no
idea what life
unfolds inside. Wind
rustles newly leafed
maples between her
and me like secrets
or charms, everyday dinner
or dishes, or long talks
or short moments of quiet
linger beyond. Mystery
itself is seductive
and wonder keeps us
true. These days roll
by and it feels right

to remember what

could be rather

than what is.

Improvisation

Days stretch longer. I packed
my sunnies but need my winter
coat. Who says we lack survival
instincts? I'm two days from 365
French lessons. Slow going, *beaucoup*
mistakes. Take the bow. I'm
writing every day this month,
which is to say, I'm writing
love letters, a stream of them, *tu me manques*
I say, as if I really spoke that tongue,
but I do—
maybe? *Qui? Pourquoi?*
The taffy-stretched sky,
fades to pink,
to purple,
midnight hued
to *bleu*. You me miss
lost somewhere in translation.

Anything Might Happen

I'm not very good
at identifying birds, most plants
or flowers, sometimes
trees. I love to walk
in nature despite
my lack of knowledge,
my sense of wonder
anything but tamped.
It can be daunting, these feelings
of not knowing, of unknowing—
I know something about some
things: dance and literature,
I can identify a Vermeer,
occasionally name a composer
from a snippet of music.
Still, I can't identify rocks,
or make jam, or tell you
who won the World Series
in any given year. But some nights
I might witness a storm blow through
in awe, watch branches tumble

down the street like acrobats
endlessly flipping, as if
everything I don't know simply
thundered through. Afterwards,
the cool night, clean and wet, smells
fresh like anything might happen
and I will know my own heart.

Rings of Saturn

My dog's golden fur seemed a deeper shade
in the snow. Her paws hurt from the bitter
cold, too much for her, too much
for me. Her face has whitened
the way dogs do when they age,
and I know I will lose her just as I
have lost others and how someone
might lose me. My hair is turning
white, not gray, the dark and light
strands create an optical illusion. Like youth,
or beauty, or the snow, which will, come
spring, melt into platters of mud. Yet
I love the snow, this slowing.
We plod through the thick of it, brilliant,
almost blinding if you let it. We plod along,
the only sound in the quiet neighborhood,
except the occasional sighs of the wind.
We round a corner, take the straight way
home, my old dog sliding into the thick
white, and then rolling, paws in the air,
a kind of revelry

before she seeks the warmth of the house, a tasty
treat, and I might wonder why I don't drop
into the white and roll, too, make snow angels
like a child. I wouldn't easily get up, but I laugh
at the idea of it. I remember walking to my car
across a blustery parking lot, only a few days before,
and a kid, couldn't have been twenty,
pointed to a brightness in the sky. "It's not
a star, it's Saturn," he said. And I like to think
my old dog looked up as she rolled and saw
bright Saturn in the winter's sky. Maybe
one night, we'll walk right through the neighborhood
and into the black, pass all the dim stars,
to the rings of that bright Saturn, staring
back at all that is wonderful and still and cold on Earth.

Glow

Author's Afterword

To say that narrative medicine changed the way I write doesn't fully encapsulate what its practice has done for me as a writer—perhaps because it changed how I write by changing me. I wrote in the shadows of other people's texts, in the company of others writing under those conditions, too. We wrote in this company to find and share what had been locked inside of us.

As I learned more about narrative medicine, I became a better version of myself, and this writing bears witness to that transformation. If stories truly underpin our human experience and our understanding of life, death, and how we navigate illness and everyday existence, then the attention to story implicit in narrative medicine opened my ability to receive, absorb, and interpret experience through writing in a way no other kind of writing had done in the past. Writing was no longer something to be consumed, but part of a long continuum of human experience. It made me more compassionate toward others and myself, better able to grapple with both what I understand and what remains forever beyond my grasp, and to let myself be awed by the mystery of attention and practice.

I worked for two years in a bustling chemotherapy infusion clinic in Morgantown, West Virginia, while my brother Nate lived with metastatic colon cancer. I worked on stories with patients as he underwent the same treatments and experiences they did, and it opened my heart to them and to him. To be a patient is to exist in a strange duality; you are both who you were before diagnosis and who you become after. I lost my brother in the first week of June 2019, and these poems, along with many others, not only helped me process that loss but kept me connected to the life I led before he died and the one I've been living since. Of all the things we cannot choose in this life, we *can* be intentional about how we connect with our essential life force. For me, that connection happens through writing, and narrative medicine has become part of my writing's wellspring.

Many of these poems began as pieces written in narrative medicine sessions, never intended for publication. In those sessions, our group would encounter a text—often poems or other writing, but sometimes visual art, music, or other expressive forms. We would give our attention over to these works through close reading, viewing, or listening, wrestling together with their meanings, subtleties, and wonder. We paid careful attention to both the work itself and each other's insights, enriching our understanding through collective effort. After this meaning-making portion of a session, participants wrote to prompts crafted with the original selection in mind—not direct responses, but thematically linked explorations that gently probed how the text affected us. These exercises teased out what lived inside participants through connections forged in deep engagement with the original work.

That many of these poems emerged from narrative medicine sessions doesn't surprise me. They continued working on me long after those sessions ended, and through ongoing engagement and careful revision—literally re-seeing—they became shapely, potent, and resonant beyond their initial form. Many nascent writings never progress past the narrative medicine session, which is also a valid outcome. They serve the exercise's purpose and the triad we strive for in our sessions: attention, representation, and affiliation. Those that move beyond perhaps kept asking questions that demanded my continued attention.

Other poems came from different wellsprings but shared common ground with those born through narrative medicine. Many are tethered to West Virginia and the Appalachian region where I live, where much of my family lives or has lived, and where I love to roam. Although I grew up largely as part of the Appalachian diaspora, living elsewhere, this was the place I came to be with family and has been my home for over twenty years, and the place I've made my home for the longest span of time. My family traces back seven generations in what was Virginia, now West Virginia, over

230 years. It's a complicated place, full of natural beauty but also destruction of that beauty in the name of commerce and progress. I don't know if my forbearers carried what we now call Appalachian fatalism, but it's a phenomenon well-known in these parts, if not by name then by its often encompassing feeling. In many ways, these poems seek to address these ills as much as any other affliction, reclaiming a place not perfect but home. It is also a tribute to the beauty of natural spaces in the place I choose to live. I am moved and awed by mountains and rivers in ways difficult to express except through poetry.

Perhaps that's how it should be.

Anyone can connect with the healing implicit in these and other poems. Narrative medicine is not a rarefied practice but a democratic one, open and available to those who seek it. Writing is one of the surest ways to help mend the spirit, and with paper and pen, perhaps a journal, you can begin writing what stirs your heart, what weighs heavy upon it, what brings you joy. The page offers a wonderful space to work through what has been troubling you but resists explanation. An image might carry as much weight as—or more than—a declaration. I would be pleased if one line or part of a poem becomes something you feel compelled to write about, whether mine or anyone else's. That's where it begins. Poems are communications, and communications flow in more than one direction. As poets, we are continually in conversation with one another. I hope you will pick up the pen and carry the message forward.

Narrative Medicine Resources

Included here is a short list of resources that may be of use to you or help inspire a practice of writing. It is not exhaustive, but represents a growing source of projects, programs, and resources that have been a part of my journey in narrative medicine.

Photo: Molly Humphreys

- Podcast available on Spotify, Apple Podcasts, SoundCloud and other platforms
- Instagram: HealthcareIsHuman

Columbia University Program in Narrative Medicine

- https://www.mhe.cuimc.columbia.edu/division-narrative-medicine
- https://narrativemedicine.blog/
- https://www.theintima.org/

Lenoir-Rhyne University

- https://www.lr.edu/narrative-healthcare-certificate

Bellevue Literary Review

- https://blreview.org/

Visual Arts in Healthcare Program at Brigham & Women's Hospital

- https://www.artsinhealthcare.org/

Johns Hopkins Center for Medical Humanities and Social Medicine

- https://hopkinsmedicalhumanities.org/
- https://hopkinsmedicalhumanities.org/tendon-magazine/

Narrative Mindworks

- https://narrativemindworks.org/

Health Humanities Consortium

- https://healthhumanitiesconsortium.com/

Acknowledgments

I am grateful to the following publications and organizations for publishing my work: “Another Poem About West Virginia,” Lost River Heart,” and “Diagnosis Color-By-Number” in *Anthology of Appalachian Writers,* 2025; “Diagnosis Color-By-Number” at *The Creative Process*, “Shenandoah Valley Gold,” “Upon Watching *North By Northwest* I Am No Longer Young,” “Diagnosis Color-By-Number,” “I Try Not To Think Of What I Might Say,” “Floats,” “Kairos,” “Can’t Find You For The Stars” “B&W Photo, 1955,” “Lost Fruit,” “1972,” “Annything Might Happen” “Rings of Saturn” and “PicturePoemRx” on the Healthcare Is Human podcast.

I am grateful for the support of the Program in Narrative Medicine at Columbia University and the community of people in and from the program who have be so supportive of my work. I am also grateful to Barrelhouse Writer Camp for giving me the time, space, and community to work on many of the poems in this collection. My Writer Camp friends are as dear and fun a writing community I will ever have.

Many of these poems got their start in narrative medicine sessions put on by Columbia’s program, and also through The Simulationists. I’m grateful to both groups for sparking my creativity and for all those involved in those sessions and this important work. I am so lucky to have these narrative medicine communities. A special thank you to Derek McCracken, who has continued to be an important part of my narrative medicine journey, and one of the best readers of poetry I’ve met. I also want to thank the health humanities scholars I work with, including Katie Rhine, Christine Bentley, Michael Stanley, Brooke DiGiovanni Evans, Aimee Mepham, Jonathan Chou, Ginny Drda and Tony Errichetti.

There were a group of women who supported me through the most painful days following the death of my brother, Nate. Thank you to Dominique Mick, Nevena Stojanovic, Stacey Culp, Dana

Huebert-Lima, Rondalyn Whitney, Rosanna Sikora, and Betsy Pyle for all the kindness and support.

Thank you to my excellent collaborators, including Sally Jane Brown, whose art brings alive the poems in this book. To my Healthcare Is Human collaborators, Ryan McCarthy, Kym Mattioli, and Molly Humphreys, thanks for all the work we do together, the shared space, and the ongoing inspiration, and for always making my poetry part of our ongoing project. You each continue to inspire me.

Special thanks to Jay for all the early reads and edits. It made this a better book, and me a better writer.

Thank you to Sarah Rudy for her music, which never ceases to inspire me.

Thank you to West Virginia Writers, Inc. for all of the opportunities to present workshops and for the literary community. You are a tremendous group. Thanks also the Chrissie Anderson Peters, for the love and literary friendship. I'm so glad we found each other.

Thank you to John Hoppenthaler, my true and trusted mentor and friend, and to the many poets whose work continues to work on me. Thank you to Natalie Homer for all the great discussions about poetry and the writing life.

To Keegan Lester and Eleni Tauntas—we survived a pandemic and beyond. Your support and friendship kept me going, and writing, in the most difficult times, and our shared joys buoy me always.

I could never write a book without the love and support of my family. Special thanks to my parents, Connie and Nick Nicholson, to my cousins Bill and Linda Parsons, to my uncle, Paul Scott, to the memory of my brother, Nate Nicholson, and my husband, Matt Bauman. I'm grateful not only because you believe in the book but believe in me.

And heartfelt thanks to the incredible quilt of friends, writers, and others, without our shared coffees and meals, deep conversations, laughs, quiet moments, readings, and all else in my life—and therefore my written words—would be diminished.

About the Artist

Sally Jane Brown is an artist, curator, and writer currently based in Morgantown. Her artwork—including drawing, painting, and performance—explores womanhood, motherhood, and the body. She has exhibited her work in spaces nationally and in the UK. Sally has won two awards for illustration for *Intimates and Fools* and *Leaves of Absence*, both with poetry by Laura Madeline Wiseman; and recently illustrated *What We Do in the Hollows* with poetry by Renée K. Nicholson. She has participated in artist residencies in Tennessee, Pennsylvania, New Mexico, and Argentina. Sally's writing has been published in *Hyperallergic, Women's Art Journal,* and *Panorama*, among others. She has curated group shows in Omaha, Nashville, Pittsburgh, and Morgantown. She has been awarded several grants for her artistic and scholarly work and presented at multiple national arts conferences.

Sally holds a Bachelor of Arts-Studio Art, a Master of Public Administration, and a Master of Arts- Art History with a certificate in Feminist Theory. She is a former member of the College Art Association National Committee on Women in the Arts, edited the online journal *Les Femmes Folles*, and currently serves as Curator for West Virginia University Libraries, Contributing Writer for the Borshch of Art *Discover Database*, and art editor for *Thimble Literary Magazine*.

About the Author

Photo: Molly Humphreys

Renée K. Nicholson, MFA is a writer and scholar based in Morgantown, West Virginia. Her creative and academic work has appeared widely in venues such as *The Gettysburg Review*, *The Millions*, *Electric Literature*, *Poets & Writers*, and *Bellevue Literary Review*.

A past Emerging Writer-in-Residence at Penn State-Altoona, Renée recently served as director of the Humanities Center at West Virginia University (now *emerita*), where she regularly collaborated with health professionals and patients to tell authentic stories from healthcare. She was the 2018 recipient of the Susan S. Landis Award from the State of West Virginia for her work writing with patients and is a creative partner in Healthcare Is Human. In October 2024, she became Series Editor for *Connective Tissue* at WVU Press.

Renée has received grants, fellowships, and residencies from the West Virginia Commission on the Arts, the West Virginia Humanities Council, the West Virginia Clinical and Translational Science Institute, the Claude Worthington Benedum Foundation, Chateau d'Orquevaux, and other organizations. She holds a Certificate of Professional Achievement in Narrative Medicine from Columbia University.

Her poetry collections include *Postscripts* and *Roundabout Directions to Lincoln Center* as well as the art and poetry chapbook *What We Do in the Hollows* with Sally Jane Brown. Her other books include *Fierce and Delicate: Essays on Dance and Illness* and the co-edited, award-winning anthology *Bodies of Truth: Personal Narratives of Illness, Disability, and Medicine.*

She is a member of numerous professional organizations, including the National Book Critics Circle, the Health Humanities Consortium, the Association of Writers and Writing Programs, Narrative Mindworks, and the Authors Guild. For more on Renée, go to www.reneenicholson.com.

www.ingramcontent.com/pod-product-compliance
Lightning Source LLC
LaVergne TN
LVHW010625100826
845148LV00014B/3117
* 9 7 9 8 8 9 9 3 3 0 1 2 4 *